WORDS THAT SHAPED AMERICA

THE MOST POWERFUL WORDS ABOUT THE AMERICAN DREAM

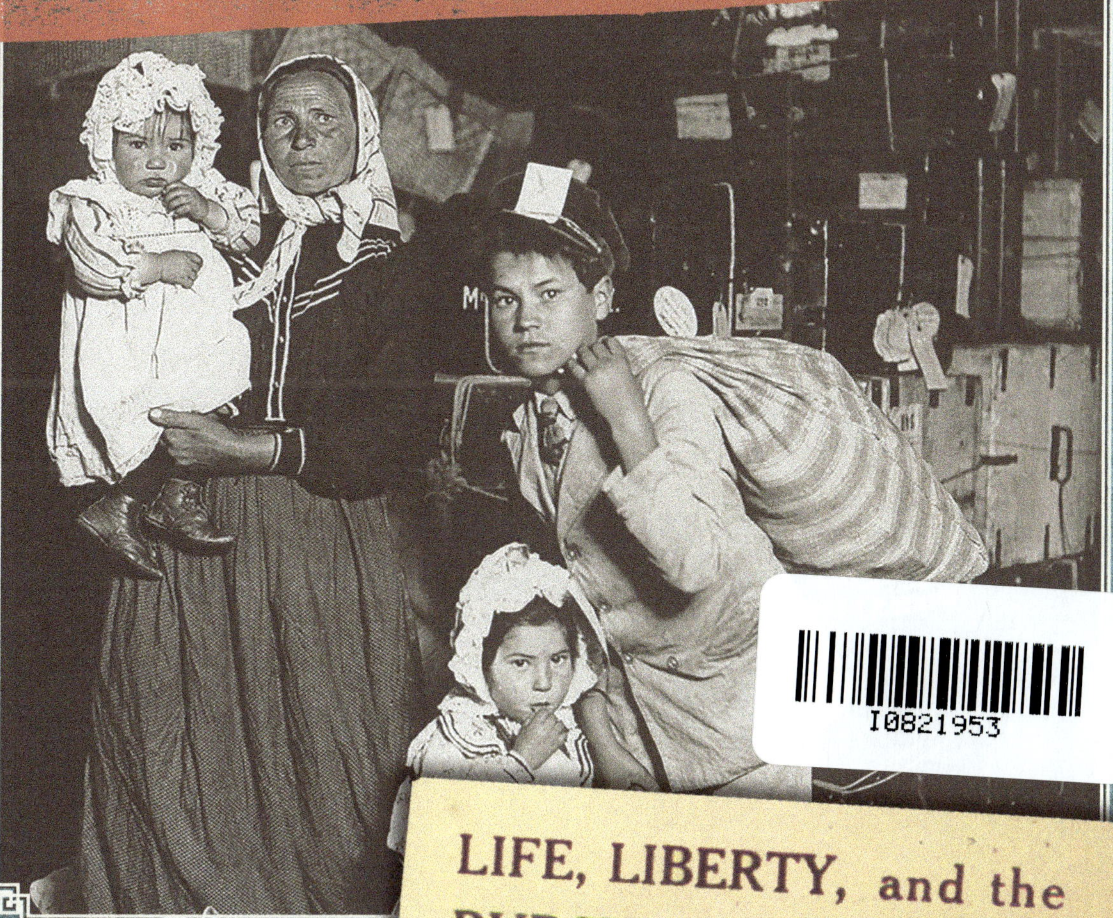

LIFE, LIBERTY, and the PURSUIT of HAPPINESS.

BY CAITIE McANENEY

Gareth Stevens PUBLISHING

Please visit our website, www.garethstevens.com. For a free color catalog of all our high-quality books, call toll free 1-800-542-2595 or fax 1-877-542-2596.

Cataloging-in-Publication Data

Names: McAneney, Caitie.
Title: The most powerful words about the American dream / Caitie McAneney.
Description: New York : Gareth Stevens Publishing, 2020. | Series: Words that shaped America | Includes glossary and index.
Identifiers: ISBN 9781538248034 (pbk.) | ISBN 9781538248058 (library bound) | ISBN 9781538248041 (6 pack)
Subjects: LCSH: American Dream--Juvenile literature. | Success--United States--Juvenile literature. | Social values--United States--Juvenile literature.
Classification: LCC HN59.2 M39 2020 | DDC 306.0973'0905--dc23

First Edition

Published in 2020 by
Gareth Stevens Publishing
111 East 14th Street, Suite 349
New York, NY 10003

Designer: Sarah Liddell
Editor: Therese Shea

Photo credits: Cover, p. 1 (main) Rich Farmbrough/Wikimedia Commons; cover, p. 1 (inset) US National Archives bot/Wikimedia Commons; ink smear used throughout Itsmesimon/Shutterstock.com; border used throughout igorrita/Shutterstock.com; background used throughout Lukasz Szwaj/Shutterstock.com; p. 5 (Horatio Alger) Transcendental Graphics/Contributor/Archive Photos/Getty Images; p. 5 (Pilgrims) P. S. Burton/Wiimedia Commons; p. 7 (Gettysburg Address) Everett Historical/Shutterstock.com; p. 7 (Declaration of Independence) Parhamr/Wikimedia Commons; p. 8 File Upload Bot (Magnus Manske)/Wikimedia Commons; p. 9 Gregg Brown/Contributor/Getty Images News/Getty Images; p. 10 H-stt/Wikimedia Commons; p. 11 Jon Brenneis/Contributor/The LIFE Images Collection/Getty Images; p. 13 Πrate/Wikimedia Commons; p. 15 (button) IagoQnsi/Wikimedia Commons; pp. 15 (Levittown), 17, 21 Bettmann/Contributor/Bettmann/Getty Images; p. 18 Coffeeandcrumbs/Wikimedia Commons; p. 19 Paul Schutzer/Contributor/The LIFE Picture Collection/Getty Images; p. 23 Michael Rougier/Contributor/The LIFE Picture Collection/Getty Images; p. 25 (Obama) Jatkins/Wikimedia Commons; p. 25 (Yes, We Can) Eric Thayer/Stringer/Getty Images News/Getty Images; p. 27 (Jazz Jennings) Emma McIntyre/Getty Images Entertainment/Getty Images; p. 27 (Emma Gonzáles) Noam Galai/Contributor/WireImage/Getty Images.

Printed in the United States of America

CPSIA compliance information: Batch #CW20GS: For further information contact Gareth Stevens, New York, New York at 1-800-542-2595.

CONTENTS

Dreaming the American Dream 4

The Pursuit of Happiness 6

A Dream of Freedom 8

A Dream of American Land 10

Coming to America 12

A Dream of Wealth 14

A Dream of Democracy 16

Civil Rights and the American Dream 18

America, the Great Society 20

Dreaming for Others 22

Reclaiming the American Dream 24

The Voice of a New Generation 26

Diversity and the American Dream 28

Glossary 30

For More Information 31

Index 32

Words in the glossary appear in **bold** type the first time they are used in the text.

DREAMING THE AMERICAN DREAM

For hundreds of years, people have traveled to America in search of a better life. America held the hope of religious freedom for the Pilgrims who arrived in 1620. The wild, open country seemed to offer many other opportunities for those who followed. Over the next four centuries, **immigrants** continued to journey to America, and to the United States, to chase what became known as the American Dream.

The "American Dream" is a term first used by author James Truslow Adams. In his book *The Epic of America*, published in 1931, Adams defined the American Dream as "that dream of a land in which life should be better and richer and fuller for every man, with opportunity for each according to ability or achievement."

BEHIND THE WORDS

MANY PEOPLE HAVE WRITTEN AND SPOKEN ABOUT THE AMERICAN DREAM OVER THE YEARS. WE CAN UNDERSTAND WHAT IT MEANS, THEN AND NOW, THROUGH THEIR WORDS.

HORATIO ALGER

Horatio Alger was a 19th-century American author who published 123 works. Many of his books were aimed at young readers and featured fictional people who rose from "rags to riches" through hard work. In Alger's works, a person's character was their most valuable feature, and with great character, one could achieve far beyond the life they were born into. To many, the "rags to riches" story represents the heart of the American Dream.

MANY CAME TO AMERICA BELIEVING IT WAS A LAND OF ECONOMIC OPPORTUNITIES AND OFTEN TO ESCAPE DIFFICULT CONDITIONS IN THEIR OWN COUNTRIES.

THE PURSUIT OF HAPPINESS

The Founding Fathers of the United States helped define the values of their new country when they drew up the Declaration of Independence in 1776. The Declaration was an official statement declaring that the American colonies were breaking from England in order to form a new country.

The Declaration of Independence states: "We hold these truths to be self-evident, that all men are created equal, that they are endowed by their Creator with certain unalienable Rights, that among these are Life, Liberty, and the pursuit of Happiness." This quote means that all Americans are born with certain rights that are unalienable, or unable to be taken away, including the ability to live freely and work toward their own happiness, which are key parts of the American Dream.

BEHIND THE WORDS

THOMAS JEFFERSON, THE DECLARATION OF INDEPENDENCE'S MAIN AUTHOR, BORROWED THE IDEA THAT PEOPLE HAVE THE RIGHT TO PURSUE HAPPINESS FROM **PHILOSOPHER** JOHN LOCKE, WHO BORROWED IT FROM GREEK PHILOSOPHERS, INCLUDING ARISTOTLE.

THE DECLARATION OF INDEPENDENCE WAS ADOPTED ON JULY 4, 1776. IT WAS GROUNDBREAKING, BUT STILL INCLUDED ONLY WHITE MALES IN ITS PROMISES.

ACHIEVING EQUALITY

The Declaration of Independence called for equality, but many people in the United States remained slaves. In President Abraham Lincoln's Gettysburg Address of 1863, he said, "Fourscore and seven years ago our fathers brought forth, on this continent, a new nation, conceived in liberty, and dedicated to the proposition that all men are created equal." Lincoln's speech suggested those who died in the Civil War brought the nation closer to that proposition, or idea, that "all men are created equal."

A DREAM OF FREEDOM

Freedom has long been a celebrated part of the American Dream. The United States is often known as the "land of the free." This line is familiar to Americans because it is from the national **anthem**, "The Star-Spangled Banner," which is often sung at sports events, like football and baseball games.

Francis Scott Key wrote the song, originally a poem called "The Defence of Fort M'Henry," in 1814. Key was inspired during the War of 1812, when he saw the US flag flying high above Fort McHenry after a British attack. He asks, "O say, does that star-spangled banner yet wave o'er the land of the free and the home of the brave?" Later in the poem, he confirms the flag *was* still waving "o'er the land of the free," a symbol of the American spirit.

FORT McHENRY

LAND OF THE FREE?

For some, the United States isn't the "land of the free." In 2019, the band The Killers released a song called "Land of the Free." In it, the band sings about political issues, such as immigration laws, gun violence, and **racism**. The song's chorus repeats "land of the free" over and over, asking listeners to consider if the United States actually is or if some US policies oppose freedom.

The national anthem and flag unify Americans, especially in times of tragedy. In this photo, the US flag hangs over the ruins of the 9/11 attacks in New York City.

BEHIND THE WORDS

"The Star-Spangled Banner" became the national anthem of the United States in 1931.

A DREAM OF AMERICAN LAND

Some immigrants sought the American Dream in the country's open landscape, especially in the West. Through the Homestead Act of 1862, settlers were promised 160 acres (65 ha) of land if they settled in the western United States. It was a chance for people who had been too poor to own land to achieve their idea of the American Dream.

Famous **conservationist** John Muir immigrated to the United States from Scotland in 1849. Muir's American Dream wasn't about owning land but about being able to enjoy America's abundant natural resources. He wrote in his book *The Story of My Boyhood and Youth*, "No other wild country I have ever known extended a kinder welcome to poor immigrants." The nation's beautiful landscape was open for everyone to experience, even those without wealth or connections.

JOHN MUIR

BEHIND THE WORDS

IN MUIR'S BOOK *OUR NATIONAL PARKS*, HE WROTE ABOUT HOW VALUABLE NATURE IS: "THOUSANDS OF TIRED, NERVE-SHAKEN, OVER-CIVILIZED PEOPLE ARE BEGINNING TO FIND OUT THAT GOING TO THE MOUNTAINS IS GOING HOME; THAT WILDNESS IS A NECESSITY."

THE AMERICAN DREAM OF LAND OWNERSHIP HAD A COST. WHILE THE HOMESTEAD ACT OF 1862 OFFERED LAND TO MANY AMERICANS, IT FORCED NATIVE AMERICANS OFF THEIR ANCESTRAL LANDS.

INTO THE WILD

John Muir is known as one of the great nature lovers of American history. He walked from Indianapolis, Indiana, to the Gulf of Mexico and sailed up the West Coast. He fell in love with California and explored the Sierra Nevada mountain range. He published 10 books and around 300 articles about his travels and played a large part in Yosemite becoming a national park in 1890. Muir is sometimes called the "Father of Our National Park System."

COMING TO AMERICA

Between the years 1892 and 1954, more than 12 million immigrants came to the United States through Ellis Island. They came for many different reasons—freedom, escape, poverty—and many were hoping to start over, chasing their American Dream. One of the first things these immigrants saw as they sailed into New York Harbor was the Statue of Liberty.

The base of the Statue of Liberty holds a poem by Jewish-American poet Emma Lazarus, which welcomes immigrants to the United States. It reads, in part:

> "Give me your tired, your poor, Your huddled masses yearning to breathe free, The wretched refuse of your teeming shore. Send these, the homeless, tempest-tost to me, I lift my lamp beside the golden door!"

The poem makes a point to welcome all those who had endured hard lives in other countries.

HOPE AND HEARTBREAK

For many immigrants, Ellis Island was a place of great hope. For others, it was a place of heartbreak. After the long journey across the Atlantic Ocean, immigrants were screened with a series of tests. They had to pass medical exams to make sure they weren't bringing in illnesses. They were asked questions about their wealth and their past as well. If they were found to be ill or a risk to the country in some way, they could be sent home.

THIS ARTWORK SHOWS IMMIGRANTS LOOKING AT THE STATUE OF LIBERTY AS THEY ARRIVE AT ELLIS ISLAND.

BEHIND THE WORDS

THE STATUE OF LIBERTY WAS A GIFT FROM FRANCE TO THE UNITED STATES, A SIGN OF FRIENDSHIP. HOWEVER, IT BECAME A WELCOMING SYMBOL TO IMMIGRANTS BECAUSE OF ITS LOCATION NEAR ELLIS ISLAND.

A DREAM OF WEALTH

In the 1920s, there was a great economic boom, which led many to redefine the American Dream. For these people, wealth and possessions became a new goal.

F. Scott Fitzgerald captured this idea in his 1925 novel, *The Great Gatsby*. The main character, Jay Gatsby, throws huge parties and lives in a large mansion, but always strives to have *more*. In one scene, Fitzgerald writes, "[Gatsby] stretched out his arms toward the dark water in a curious way, and, far as I was from him, I could have sworn he was trembling. Involuntarily I glanced seaward—and distinguished nothing except a single green light." The green light is a symbol of Gatsby's hopes and dreams. Though he'd achieved his American Dream, it was not enough to make him happy. He was reaching for more.

BEHIND THE WORDS

F. SCOTT FITZGERALD KNEW THE WORLD OF *THE GREAT GATSBY* WELL. HE USED HIS OWN EXPERIENCE LIVING THROUGH THE ROARING TWENTIES, OR THE JAZZ AGE, WHEN WRITING THE BOOK, WHICH WAS PUBLISHED IN 1925.

ECONOMIC BOOMS

Economic booms in the United States have often resulted in a greater emphasis on materialism, or a focus on goods and possessions. For example, the boom in the 1950s, after World War II, allowed more people to hold jobs and buy houses, cars, and other products. When US presidents Ronald Reagan and Donald Trump used the saying, "Make America Great Again," they were referring to economic booms of the nation's past.

LET'S MAKE AMERICA GREAT AGAIN
REAGAN '80

After World War II, millions of Americans moved from cities to suburbs. Millions of homes were built, such as this development in Levittown, New York. Owning a home became an achievable part of the American dream for many.

A DREAM OF DEMOCRACY

In 1961, former first lady Eleanor Roosevelt wrote an article in the magazine *The Atlantic* called "What Has Happened to the American Dream?" In it, she said that Americans had gotten away from democratic ideals. She called on young Americans to be representatives of democracy to the world, to respect other countries, and to lead by example.

Roosevelt wrote: "The future will be determined by the young, and there is no more essential task today, it seems to me, than to bring before them once more, in all its brightness, in all its splendor and beauty, the American Dream, lest we let it fade, too concerned with ways of earning a living or impressing our neighbors or getting ahead or finding bigger and more potent [powerful] ways of destroying the world and all that is in it."

BEHIND THE WORDS

A DEMOCRACY IS A SYSTEM OF GOVERNMENT IN WHICH CITIZENS HAVE A VOICE IN GOVERNMENT. THEY CHOOSE THEIR LEADERS THROUGH FAIR ELECTIONS.

ELEANOR ROOSEVELT WROTE, "THERE IS THE MOST TREMENDOUS ADVENTURE IN BRINGING THE PEOPLES OF THE WORLD TO AN UNDERSTANDING OF THE AMERICAN DREAM."

DEMOCRATIC IDEALS

Eleanor Roosevelt believed that the American Dream was a way of life that could be achieved only through democracy. She worried that Americans were forgetting democracy's value and missing out on the opportunity to spread it to other countries. Roosevelt wrote the article after learning that Russia sent its youth into developing nations with **communist** ideals. She believed young Americans, too, should go out into the world and spread democratic ideals—and the idea of the American Dream.

CIVIL RIGHTS AND THE AMERICAN DREAM

In the 1950s and 1960s, a civil rights movement started in the United States. Although slavery had been outlawed around 100 years before, African Americans were still suffering from **segregation** and **discrimination**. In many places, they didn't have the benefits of freedom and equality—or the ability to pursue the American Dream.

One of the leaders of the civil rights movement was Dr. Martin Luther King Jr. He delivered his "I Have a Dream" speech at the March on Washington on August 28, 1963. One of the speech's most famous lines is: "I have a dream that my four little children will one day live in a nation where they will not be judged by the color of their skin but by the content of their character." The movement made important advances under King's leadership.

MARTIN LUTHER KING JR.

MARTIN LUTHER KING JR.

Martin Luther King Jr. was born in 1929 in Atlanta, Georgia. He was a Baptist minister and a powerful speaker who became the head of the Southern Christian Leadership Conference (SCLC). The SCLC worked for civil rights, and with King at the wheel, practiced nonviolence to achieve their goals. They would organize peaceful protests like sit-ins, where African Americans sat at segregated food counters and refused to leave. King won the Nobel Peace Prize in 1964 but was assassinated, or killed, in 1968.

THE AMERICAN DREAM OF EQUALITY AND CIVIL RIGHTS WAS WORTH FIGHTING FOR. ABOUT 250,000 PEOPLE GATHERED IN FRONT OF THE LINCOLN MEMORIAL IN WASHINGTON, DC, FOR THE MARCH ON WASHINGTON.

BEHIND THE WORDS

MARTIN LUTHER KING JR. USED THE WORDS OF THE DECLARATION OF INDEPENDENCE IN HIS SPEECH WHEN HE SAID: "I HAVE A DREAM THAT ONE DAY THIS NATION WILL RISE UP AND LIVE OUT THE TRUE MEANING OF ITS CREED: 'WE HOLD THESE TRUTHS TO BE SELF-EVIDENT, THAT ALL MEN ARE CREATED EQUAL.'"

AMERICA, THE GREAT SOCIETY

On May 22, 1964, President Lyndon B. Johnson delivered his famous "Great Society" speech. At the University of Michigan, Johnson spoke about the importance of using America's wealth to advance American civilization. He said, "For in your time, we have the opportunity to move not only toward the rich society and the powerful society, but upward to the Great Society. The Great Society rests on abundance and liberty for all. It demands an end to poverty and racial injustice, to which we are totally committed in our time."

Johnson's "Great Society" focused on improving and rebuilding cities, protecting nature, and educating all children. His vision of the American Dream was a place where all people, regardless of race or social class, could be free and able to prosper.

BEHIND THE WORDS

IN 1964, LYNDON B. JOHNSON SIGNED THE CIVIL RIGHTS ACT, WHICH MADE SEGREGATION IN PUBLIC PLACES AND DISCRIMINATION IN JOBS AND SCHOOLS ILLEGAL.

LIKE ELEANOR ROOSEVELT, LYNDON B. JOHNSON CALLED ON YOUNG PEOPLE TO MAKE A DIFFERENCE IN AMERICA AND HELP ALL PEOPLE ACHIEVE THE AMERICAN DREAM.

"UGLY AMERICA"

In another part of Lyndon Johnson's speech, he said, "A few years ago we were greatly concerned about the 'Ugly American.' Today we must act to prevent an ugly America." Eleanor Roosevelt had described an Ugly American as one who behaves badly in other countries and disrespects other cultures. Johnson's "Ugly America" referred to Americans ruining their water, shores, parks, and forests. As part of the Great Society, he wanted to save the "natural splendor" of America.

DREAMING FOR OTHERS

To many, the American Dream means achieving justice for *all* people. In the 1960s and 1970s, Cesar Chavez worked to make the dream possible for the **disadvantaged**. The son of Mexican immigrants, Chavez had worked in the farm fields of California from a young age. He saw the unfair and poor conditions faced by migrant workers—racism, crowded camps, and low wages. He led the National Farm Workers Association, fighting for rights for farm workers across America.

Chavez was also a leader of a Mexican American (Chicano) civil rights movement of the 1960s. He said, "We cannot seek achievement for ourselves and forget about progress and prosperity for our community. . . . Our ambitions must be broad enough to include the aspirations [desires] and needs of others, for their sakes and for our own."

BEHIND THE WORDS

MILLIONS OF PEOPLE LIVING IN THE UNITED STATES ARE **UNDOCUMENTED** AND FEAR BEING DEPORTED, OR SENT BACK TO THE COUNTRIES THEY'VE LEFT.

THE DREAM ACT

People are still fighting for rights for undocumented immigrants, especially those from Latin American countries. The DREAM Act (which stands for Development, Relief, and Education for Alien Minors) was a proposed program through which people who were brought to the United States as children could become legal citizens and have a shot at the American Dream. These people are known as DREAMers. The DREAM Act never passed in the federal government, though several states have passed similar acts.

CESAR CHAVEZ BELIEVED IN NONVIOLENT PROTESTS. HERE, HE'S PICTURED WITH SENATOR ROBERT KENNEDY AFTER ENDURING A HUNGER STRIKE FOR 25 DAYS.

RECLAIMING THE AMERICAN DREAM

Barack Obama was the first African American president of the United States. He was a sign of hope and unity for many Americans. Obama promised to fight for his idea of the American Dream for every American, regardless of race or class. He wanted everyone to get an education, receive a fair wage, and have health care.

In a 2007 speech, Obama announced his "American Dream Agenda." He said: "America is the sum of our dreams. And what binds us together, what makes us one American family, is that we stand up and fight for each other's dreams, that we reaffirm [restate] that fundamental belief . . . through our politics, our policies, and in our daily lives. It's time to reclaim the American dream."

BEHIND THE WORDS

IN 2006, BEFORE BECOMING PRESIDENT, BARACK OBAMA PUBLISHED THE BOOK *THE AUDACITY OF HOPE: THOUGHTS ON RECLAIMING THE AMERICAN DREAM.*

"YES, WE CAN"

Barack Obama's presidential campaign slogan was "Yes, We Can." In his victory speech, he said: "This is our time . . . to reclaim the American dream and reaffirm that fundamental truth, that, out of many, we are one; that while we breathe, we hope. And where we are met with **cynicism** and doubts and those who tell us that we can't, we will respond with that timeless creed that sums up the spirit of a people: Yes, we can."

To many, Barack Obama was an example of the American dream. He rose from humble beginnings and was elected to the nation's highest office.

THE VOICE OF A NEW GENERATION

The speeches and writings of the Founding Fathers, presidents, and leaders of cultural movements have shaped the American Dream of the past. However, the words of the newest generation will shape the future of the American Dream.

The *New York Times* asked students what the American Dream meant to them. High school student Caitlyn Pellerin said the American Dream was people of different **ethnicities**, religions, and sexual orientations all having the equal chance to climb the ladder of success without discrimination. She answered: "As we progress in our efforts for true equality and lack of prejudices, I have hope that my generation will be able to make this not only the American Dream, but the American reality."

BEHIND THE WORDS

TRANSGENDER TEEN JAZZ JENNINGS WROTE ABOUT HER DREAM FOR THE FUTURE IN HER BOOK *BEING JAZZ*: "CHANGE HAPPENS THROUGH UNDERSTANDING, AND ONE OF MY BIGGEST HOPES IS THAT OUR NEXT GENERATION OF KIDS WILL GROW UP IN A WORLD WITH MORE COMPASSION."

YOUNG PEOPLE FIND THEIR VOICE

Young people are fighting for their own American Dreams, taking on issues such as climate change and LGBTQ+ rights. In 2018, Emma Gonzáles, survivor of a shooting at her high school in Parkland, Florida, spoke about gun control at the March for Our Lives. That same year, DREAMer Sandy Rivera addressed the Women's March in Indiana about immigration. She said: "We must continue to fight for those who live in the shadows. We must continue to fight for those without voice."

EMMA GONZÁLES

JAZZ JENNINGS

SOME STUDIES FIND THAT YOUNG PEOPLE ARE UNSURE IF THE TRADITIONAL AMERICAN DREAM OF WEALTH AND PROSPERITY IS POSSIBLE ANYMORE. MANY, LIKE EMMA GONZÁLES, FIGHT FOR A FUTURE WHERE AMERICA IS A SAFE, OPEN SPACE FOR ALL PEOPLE.

DIVERSITY AND THE AMERICAN DREAM

US Senator Kamala Harris said, "The American Dream belongs to all of us." But for most of US history, reaching the American Dream wasn't possible for all. Civil rights, labor, and social movements fought to make it achievable for more Americans.

Diversity is now a core part of the nation's identity and the new face of the American Dream. Former US Secretary of Labor Thomas Perez said, "Our workforce and our entire economy are strongest when we embrace diversity to its fullest, and that means opening doors of opportunity to everyone and recognizing that the American Dream excludes no one." Embracing diversity and respecting each other strengthens our entire nation—and makes the American Dream open to more people than ever before.

BEHIND THE WORDS

IN 2019, A REPORT FOUND THAT AMERICANS TODAY VALUE THE "FREEDOM OF CHOICE IN HOW TO LIVE" OVER WEALTH, CAREER, AND SUCCESS.

DIVERSITY IN AMERICA

America is becoming more and more diverse. As of 2017, non-Hispanic whites make up the greatest portion of the population, but other ethnic groups are on the rise. Black, Asian, and Hispanic populations are growing faster than the white population, and the number of people who identify as biracial is on the rise. Experts think there will be more Americans from minority groups than white Americans by 2045.

AN AMERICAN DREAM TIMELINE

1776: THE DECLARATION OF INDEPENDENCE PROMISES A GOVERNMENT THAT SUPPORTS "THE PURSUIT OF HAPPINESS."

1815: WAVES OF EUROPEAN IMMIGRANTS ENTER THE UNITED STATES.

1862: THE HOMESTEAD ACT OFFERS WESTERN LAND TO AMERICANS.

1892: ELLIS ISLAND OPENS AS AN IMMIGRATION INSPECTION STATION.

1925: F. SCOTT FITZGERALD'S *THE GREAT GATSBY* IS PUBLISHED.

1962: CESAR CHAVEZ FORMS THE NATIONAL FARM WORKERS ASSOCIATION TO IMPROVE CONDITIONS FOR FARM WORKERS.

1963: DR. MARTIN LUTHER KING JR. DELIVERS HIS "I HAVE A DREAM" SPEECH AT THE MARCH ON WASHINGTON.

1964: LYNDON B. JOHNSON GIVES HIS "GREAT SOCIETY" SPEECH.

2001: THE DREAM ACT IS PROPOSED, BUT FAILS TO PASS.

2007: BARACK OBAMA ANNOUNCES HIS "AMERICAN DREAM AGENDA."

2019: THE AMERICAN ENTERPRISE INSTITUTE AND THE NORC RESEARCH CENTER REPORTS "FREEDOM OF CHOICE IN HOW TO LIVE" IS VALUED BY AMERICANS OVER WEALTH, CAREER, AND SUCCESS.

GLOSSARY

anthem: a song declaring loyalty to a group, cause, or country

communist: having to do with a system in which the government owns the things that are used to make and transport products and there is no privately owned property

conservationist: a person concerned with conservation, or the care of nature

cynicism: the belief that people are selfish and dishonest

disadvantaged: lacking things that are necessary for an equal position in society

discrimination: unfairly treating people unequally because of their race or beliefs

diversity: the state of having different races or cultures of people in a community

ethnicity: a part of a person's identity based on where they or their family come from

immigrant: one who comes to a country to settle there

philosopher: a person who tries to discover and understand the nature of knowledge

racism: the belief that people of different races have different qualities and abilities and that some are superior or inferior

segregation: the forced separation of races or classes

transgender: having to do with a person whose true nature does not match their sex at birth

undocumented: not having the official documents that are needed to enter, live in, or work in a country legally

FOR MORE INFORMATION

BOOKS

Carney, Elizabeth. *Ellis Island*. Washington, DC: National Geographic, 2016.

Muhammad, Ibtihaj. *Proud: Living My American Dream*. New York, NY: Little, Brown and Company, 2018.

WEBSITES

Barack Obama
www.brainpop.com/socialstudies/famoushistoricalfigures/barackobama/
Learn more about the life of the first African American president of the United States.

Civil Rights
www.ducksters.com/history/civil_rights/african-american_civil_rights_movement.php
Explore the American civil rights movement and meet some of the leaders that changed America.

What Is Diversity?
www.cyh.com/HealthTopics/HealthTopicDetailsKids.aspx?p=335&np=286&id=2345
Learn more about diversity, and how you can accept and celebrate the differences between you and others.

Publisher's note to educators and parents: Our editors have carefully reviewed these websites to ensure that they are suitable for students. Many websites change frequently, however, and we cannot guarantee that a site's future contents will continue to meet our high standards of quality and educational value. Be advised that students should be closely supervised whenever they access the internet.

INDEX

Adams, James Truslow 4

Alger, Horatio 5

Chavez, Cesar 22, 23, 29

Civil Rights Act of 1964 20

Declaration of Independence 6, 7, 29

DREAM Act 23, 29

DREAMers 23

Ellis Island 12, 13, 29

The Epic of America 4

Fitzgerald, F. Scott 14, 29

Gettysburg Address 7

González, Emma 27

The Great Gatsby 14, 29

The Great Society 20, 21, 29

Harris, Kamala 28

Homestead Act of 1862 10, 29

Jazz Age 14

Jefferson, Thomas 6, 7

Jennings, Jazz 26, 27

Johnson, Lyndon B. 20, 21, 29

Key, Francis Scott 8

King, Martin Luther, Jr. 18, 19

Lazarus, Emma 12

Lincoln, Abraham 7

March on Washington 18, 19

Muir, John 10, 11

National Farm Workers Association (NFWA) 22

Obama, Barack 24, 25, 29

Pellerin, Caitlyn 26

Perez, Thomas 28

Pilgrims 4

Roaring Twenties 14

Roosevelt, Eleanor 16, 17, 21

Southern Christian Leadership Conference (SCLC) 19

"The Star-Spangled Banner" 8, 9

Statue of Liberty 12, 13

suburbs 15

Yosemite 11